WHEN

HAPPENS

MINDY MILLS MAYNARD

*The views and opinions expressed in this book are solely those of the author and do not necessarily reflect the views and opinions of the publisher.*

*For My Daughter*

ALEXANDRIA THERESA LALLY MAYNARD

who has made my life magical.

*Photo by Mindy Mills Maynard*

# ABOUT THE COVER

*T*HIS IS WHERE I LIKE TO START MY DAY. I have lived in East Hampton, Connecticut for a majority of my life. At the age of 23, I moved here from the Connecticut shoreline with my husband. We bought a condo on the shore of Lake Pocotopaug. We had our own private beach and boat docks. I quickly made use of both. The first year we lived here, this tree took a beating during Hurricane Gloria and has a huge scar where a branch had broken off. Not only did we spend our summers here swimming, fishing, sun tanning and boating, we also enjoyed the other seasons here, especially winter. We would go ice skating when the lake was frozen solid. I have walked across the frozen lake three times.

My daughter spent many years under this tree or playing on that rock, either sleeping in her stroller in the shade or having wild adventures with her Beanie Babies and Ariel, the mermaid Barbie. That rock is the perfect place for me to sit for sunrise as it has a spot that my behind fits in perfectly.

Both tree and rock have symbolic meaning for me. This tree is my Tree of Life, it fills my soul with energy and hope for the future. The rock reminds me to stay strong. Together, they have weathered many storms over the years and made it through. Changed, yes, but still standing.

I am blessed for this spot and all the memories and beauty it has given me for so many years. With all its peacefulness here at sunrise, it offers a great start to the day, a new beginning (even if only 10°!) with hope. Its brilliance reminds me that out of darkness comes light and another chance for MAGIC to happen.

"THERE'S A FLAME OF MAGIC inside every stone & every flower, every bird that sings & every frog that croaks. There's magic in the trees & the hills & the river & the rocks, in the sea & the stars & the wind, a deep, wild magic that's as old as the world itself. It's in you too, my darling ..., and in me, and in every living creature, be it ever so small. Even the dirt I'm sweeping up now is stardust. In fact, all of us are made from the stuff of stars!"

~ K. FORSYTH

# CONTENTS

### AFTERWARD

 *Chapter* 1

# THE MOTORCYCLE MAN

"MAGIC WILL FIND those with pure hearts, even
when all seems lost. And love is
the greatest magic of all."

~ MORGAN RHODES

*S*INCE I WAS A YOUNG GIRL, I have been fascinated by the natural world. So "naturally," I was open to what that world held. Fairies were winged insects. Trolls and gnomes were toads and salamanders. Elves were the furry night creatures, and kings and queens, the lions, tigers and bears. Of course, the witches were snakes and bees. In the natural world, magic is happening all the time. This world captivated me so much that I became an artist to try to capture its magic. I became a professional gardener to protect the magic and give it a place to flourish.

As a young girl, I was aware of this magic that surrounded me. But, the first time I actually witnessed it right in front of my face was the most powerful magic of all. The power of LOVE! It was like a spark, or should I say a sparkle, in two people's eyes. It hit me hard as I watched love happen over a candlelit dinner table. I was 15 years old.

This story is not about how I found love, but how my mother found love!

In 1976, my parents divorced. We were living in Cleveland, Ohio at the time. In the year that my mother and father were divorcing, my mother went back to college to finish her degree. She never was able to finish her degree from the University of Georgia where she met my dad. Instead, she got married and had a baby. ME!

After graduating, she started looking at colleges down south to pursue her master's degree. As she was from Georgia and both sets of grandparents lived in Tennessee, she thought it was best that we move out of Cleveland and back to the South, back to her roots and closer to my grandparents.

She got her best offer at the University of Tennessee, and that summer we packed up the U-Haul and moved to Knoxville.

Well, we didn't last too long in Tennessee. Only a year. It was a terrible year and everything that could go wrong did go wrong! Not to mention the culture shock. We Northerners needed to get back home to where we belonged, so we planned our escape back to Cleveland!

On Memorial Day, my mother wanted to take me and my two brothers out to dinner at a nice restaurant. She had just gotten paid and felt bad that we had to go to school on a holiday. We were not having it. We wanted to go to Hardee's. We begged and pleaded with our mom. My brother even cut some coupons out of the paper for Hardee's to convince her. Finally, she caved in and off we went to Hardee's in my mom's brown Pinto Runabout.

Meanwhile, there was a motorcycle man riding his vintage motorcycle from Connecticut to the western part of Tennessee to visit his sister. The small gas tank on the vintage motorcycle only got 75 miles to the tank, so he had to make sure that he mapped out pit stops along the way. One, so he didn't run out of gas in the middle of God's country, and two, so he didn't have to backtrack. One thing he hated doing was back-tracking. The other two things that he absolutely hated were eating fast food and sitting on the sunny side of any restaurant. That day he did all three.

Having to backtrack for gas landed him in Knoxville, Tennessee, and being hungry, he stopped at Hardee's for a quick burger and sat on the sunny side of the restaurant. While there, in walked three loud teenagers and their single, divorced mom. After getting our order, we all plopped down in the booth right in front of the motorcycle man, a handsome, tank-topped muscular tattooed guy. At one point while we were eating our burgers, the motorcycle man started a conversation with our mom. He explained that he was riding his motorcycle from Connecticut to visit his sister and wanted to know where in Tennessee the time zone changed. My mom was glad to provide this information for him. They chatted a bit and they both realized they had just read the same book: The Zen and Art of Motorcycle Maintenance. That began a whole new conversation.

When we were finished eating, we said our goodbyes and bid safe travels to the motorcycle man. As we were getting in the car, we were all talking about him. How handsome and nice he was. My mom got it in her head to go back into the restaurant, give him her address, and offer him a home cooked meal on his return to Connecticut. We practically pushed our mother out of that Pinto! We watched her go into the restaurant from the car and she did just what she said she was going to do. She decided to live dangerously and let the chips fall where they may. ...

## ONE WEEK LATER

We were guessing he was not really intending to call this single mom of three teenagers. Let's face it, we were moving back to Cleveland, he lived in Connecticut. What could he be thinking? What could possibly come from it? She had three teenage kids, he had three kids of his own. But, a week later, and one day early, he stopped by! My mom was not home, but my brother was. Motorcycle Man told him he would be back in the morning to take my mom to breakfast.

He and my mom spent a lovely day together, and he stayed that evening for his home-cooked meal. I don't remember what my mom made for dinner that night, but years later she said it was probably meatloaf. During that candlelight dinner I saw magic. Magic so powerful that I saw sparks fly from the motorcycle man's eyes. They sparkled every time he looked at my mom. I knew it was love! And I got to see it happen.

We did move back to Cleveland but only for five months. During that five months, Motorcycle Man came to visit us and my mom visited him. Many love letters later, they decided to get married! We had struck gold! A bit like the Clampetts, we loaded up the U-Haul truck and moved to the Hills – of Connecticut, that is! They were married in Vermont and are still happily married 45 years later. The stars had aligned on the day they met in Tennessee under the most unlikely of circumstances, and everything changed for all of us.

## Chapter 11

# MEETING KATE

Jack in the Pulpit

"WHEN YOU TRULY LOVE YOURSELF,

magic will start to happen!"

~ K.H.

**AT A VERY YOUNG AGE** I was obsessed with old black and white movies. Every Saturday afternoon was devoted to watching old movies; Jerry Lewis, Dean Martin, Frank Sinatra, Elvis. All the big band music, all the musicals, the dancing, the costumes, everything! I was obsessed! Cary Grant was my secret Hollywood Crush. And still today, at age 60, I prefer to listen to big band music more than any other music.

When I moved to Connecticut, I settled in a small town at the mouth of the Connecticut River on Long Island Sound. A very famous actress lived in our town, or so I was told. An actress from the period that I was obsessed with. A very prominent actress. It was also rumored that she shopped in town. So, possibly getting a glimpse of this famous actress was my goal. When I was 20 years old, I worked for my soon to be in-laws at their Farmers Market on Route 1 in this little town. The summer that I worked there, my future mother-in-law told me that I would probably be seeing this very famous actress inside the Farmers Market. She only came in twice a year, once when the sugar snap peas were in season and when the Maynard's fresh corn came in. We had the best corn in town. My future mother-in-law also told me that when she came in to be calm and treat her like everyone else because she wanted to be treated like a normal customer. All summer I waited. ...

## SEVERAL WEEKS LATER

It was a hot muggy summer afternoon, and I was at the farmers market, which we fondly called, "The Stand." The summer tourists were at the beaches that afternoon, so business was quite slow, until a car pulled up, not a fancy car, just a car. Then, in walked two elderly ladies. Not really paying attention to them coming into the door, I heard a woman asking me if the corn was fresh... in a voice so distinctive that I knew exactly who the person was. I turned around quickly toward that voice and there she was and all her beautiful glory... Katherine Hepburn! I tried to remain calm, but inside I was screaming and jumping up and down for joy. I finally get to meet Katherine Hepburn! I replied it was freshly picked that day, then grabbed an ear, and peeled back part of the husk to show her that it was butter and sugar corn. She took it from my hand and promptly took a huge bite out of it! She ordered a dozen! After she left, I did a little happy dance... I met Katherine Hepburn!!

Later that summer I had a conversation with my future mother-in-law about a beautiful tree that was on their property and what kind was it? She explained to me it was an oak tree and Katherine Hepburn once told her how much she loved that tree and said she would sometimes go and just stand in front of it to look at it and be part of its glory. I loved that story about Katherine Hepburn. ...

## ONE MONTH LATER

Sitting with my soon-to-be husband watching "20/20", a news show that began in 1978. Barbara Walters was doing an interview with Katherine Hepburn. At the end of the interview, Katherine Hepburn was asked how she identified herself. She said as A TREE, to which Barbara Walters responded, "If you could be a tree, what kind of tree would you be?" Before she could answer I yelled out, "An OAK TREE!" And then Katherine Hepburn said it herself on national TV, "I would be an oak tree." My fiancé just looked at me crazy weird and asked, "How did you know that she was going to say that?" I told him about the conversation I had with his mother, and not only is she an oak tree, but she is the very oak tree that's on your brother's property right now. That's the oak tree that she identifies with. It was a magical moment. And what on earth and how on earth did Barbara Walters even think to ask her how she identifies herself followed by and what kind of tree would she be?

She didn't just come into the stand once that summer, she came in several times, and it was always a pleasure waiting on her. I always remained calm, but secretly I wish I had asked her for her autograph and gushed over her and gave her a hug. Maybe I should have. Oh, the things we wish we had done.

*Chapter* III

# DANCING WITH PATTON

# "DANCE ISN'T JUST A DANCE.

It's magical!"

~ ANONYMOUS

*M*Y GRANDFATHER, Robert Alfred Mills grew up in Cleveland. When he was 13 years old, he met the love of his life in middle school. Her name was Olive Gardener. After graduating high school he attended Georgia Tech and majored in chemical engineering. He also joined the army ROTC. After graduating Georgia Tech, he married Olive Gardener on January 2, 1939. Soon after, he joined the army and eventually participated in World War II. On a leave home, my grandmother became pregnant with their only child, Robert Walter Mills, my dad. During my grandfather's time in the war, he rose in rank to Lieutenant Colonel. He was very proud of that. Until the day he died, he carried his army card in his wallet.

After the war, he traveled across our country and parts of the world to build chemical plants. At 55, my grandfather retired and bought a 150-acre old farm in the middle of Appalachia, on top of a mountain, where there was only a dirt road up and over the mountain until the mid 80s. I have always referred to my grandparents as the couple from Green Acres, the 1970s show about a lawyer and his wife played by Eva Gabor who moved from Manhattan, New York City to some old farm in a quirky country town to live off the land. Well, that show was totally about my grandparents, and they made many friends with those down home, good ol' boy, country people even though they were straight up Northerners. They built a home, bought a tractor and grew a huge garden eventually adding a barn, a root cellar, some cattle and some ducks. Growing up, we spent every holiday or vacation with my grandparents, but after they moved to Tennessee, we went there at least two to three times a year. We packed up the station-wagon with a cooler, three kids, and our belongings for the week and we drove 12 straight hours to Tennessee from

Cleveland. Only made one stop at the border of Tennessee and Kentucky at Jellico Mountain to sit at their diner on the edge of the mountain that looked out all the way into Tennessee. It was such a great time on those road trips! When we arrived in Tennessee there was always a hearty meal waiting for us. After dessert we were ushered off into the spare bedroom so my two brothers and I could get a good night's sleep. The next week, we were going to be working.

My grandfather would wake us up every morning by whistling morning taps. That was our queue to get up and get dressed, breakfast was about to be served. On the first morning, he always pulled out his yellow pad of paper with the list of what we were going to accomplish that week. He had five able bodies to do some pretty big projects and he made sure that we stayed busy. We worked in the mornings when it was still cool. But after lunch we were free to do whatever we wanted to do. We had 150 acres of magic to do it on! Old cart paths to discover, creeks to explore, wildflowers, insects, lizards and scorpions, oh my! And, then there were the SNAKES, poisonous snakes! We were always warned to be careful of the snakes. So there was plenty for three young kids to stay busy with all afternoon. Some afternoons, I was so tired that while my brothers were off doing gosh knows what, I went to have a little nap down in the spare bedroom. One of these times I looked inside the spare bedroom closet, and I discovered some things that were covered over in plastic hanging there. Some of them were just tablecloths. One was a fancy long blue velvet dress, the other one was also blue but it was a short little cocktail dress. Every time I went to visit even into my twenties, I would go into that closet and I would crush on those dresses. …

The last time I went to visit my grandparents at the farm, I was in my early twenties, and I had confessed to my grandmother about my obsession with the two dresses. At this point, I knew that the blue velvet one was the dress my grandmother was married in, but I didn't know the stories behind the dresses. Grandma revealed that the blue velvet dress was originally the bridesmaid's dress that she wore in a wedding in the October prior to her getting married. Because her family were farmers and not well off, it was only fitting that she wore this dress to get married in. And it was her favorite color. The other dress, the little cocktail dress. …

My grandmother looked at me very proudly and said, "I danced with General Patton in that dress. I was at an officer's ball with your grandfather, and Patton was there. He asked me to dance with him."

Because my grandfather rose in rank to Lieutenant Colonel, he traveled with Patton and liberated many, many concentration camps under his command. He never talked about those times. I'm sure what he saw was horrific. So that is how they ended up at an officer's ball with General Patton. …

## 15 YEARS LATER

After my grandmother passed, I told my father the only things I wanted were the blue velvet dress, the other blue cocktail dress, and her quilt. I'm the owner of all three now along with so many more things of hers and my ancestors. It took me a while after getting the dresses before I finally, after so many years of dreaming of wearing these dresses, tried them on! To my surprise and delight, they both fit me perfectly!

 IV

# THE MOON ASHTRAY

"THE WORLD IS FULL of magic things, patiently waiting for our senses to grow sharper."

~ *W.B. YEATS*

**W**HEN MY DAUGHTER WAS NEARLY THREE, she sparked an idea in her head to do some gift-giving. She went through her toys and picked out ones she didn't play with any more, and unbeknownst to me, other items throughout the house. She gift wrapped them all and was ready to give out her gifts. I thought it was a sweet idea. But clearly I was not paying enough attention to what she was giving. Little did I know that one of the gifts was something of mine, a brass half-moon astray. This ashtray was very special to me. It was my dad's. He had gifted it to me. Now, I do not smoke, but I did have friends who visited who smoked. For years I used an old clam shell for an ashtray. I was so happy to be able to supply a very cool and functional ashtray to my guests.

That afternoon we took one of the wrapped gifts to my in-law's house. It was for her Grampy. She was so excited to give her gift. As he was opening it, I realized it was my moon ashtray. Grampy was excited to get such a cool ashtray because he did smoke. Big fat cigars. As soon as I saw the gift, I exclaimed, "Hey, that's my moon ashtray my dad gave me!" My father-in-law took one look at me and said, "Well, now it's mine." A bit confused by this response, I let it go. I figured he was just saying that in front of my daughter to not make her feel bad and would eventually give me my moon ashtray back at some point. But that's not what happened. ...

## FIVE YEARS LATER

My father-in-law never gave me back my ashtray and used it every day until he passed. It always stuck in my craw that he never gave it back. At this point, I was divorced. While my daughter was at her dads for the weekend, I had a few friends over. The smokers complained about my clam shell of an ashtray I had to resort back to using. "Yeah, yeah, yeah," I said. "I had a really cool ashtray," and I told them the story. I was still pretty mad about my ashtray! I cursed my late father-in-law and ranted about it loudly that night. …

## 12 HOURS LATER

I went to pick up my daughter on Sunday and her father handed me a used McDonald's bag and told me not to open it till I got home. Really now? What could be in that bag? Anxious to get home and a little nervous about what could be in that bag, I did as he said and waited till I got home. I opened the bag…to my great surprise was THE MOON ASHTRAY!

How he knew I was complaining about it the very night before, I don't know, but there it was in all its magical brass glory!

*Chapter* v

# CLEVELAND VS BOSTON

"MAGIC IS JUST SCIENCE
that we don't understand yet."

~ ARTHUR C. CLARKE

*I*N MY MID THIRTIES, my friend and I had a fun, friendly rivalry over the love of baseball and our teams, the Cleveland Indians, (which aren't even called the Cleveland Indians anymore!) and the Boston Red Sox. At the time, our teams were the butt of every baseball joke. We didn't mind. We were hardcore fans and we were true to our teams. Every time Cleveland and Boston played each other, I always joked to my friend about how Cleveland's going to beat Boston again.

One year, my friend suggested that we go see our teams play each other in Boston. Wow! That sounded like a great idea considering I would get to see my team beat the Boston Red Sox right on their own turf. Count me in! When spring came and the baseball schedule was made, we booked our trip to Boston. This went on for a couple years until one year we decided to invite a couple of our girlfriends to come along. Make it a girls' weekend!

At dinner that night before the ball game, I had one of my premonitions. I have been getting them since I was a teen. A flash in my brain brings up a vision and usually within the day, that vision comes true. Sometimes within seconds even. At dinner, I had one of those flashes. The vision was of a baseball being hit out to us in the stands. Instead of remaining quiet like I usually do when I have one of these visions, often it is just such a fleeting thought in my head and then it's gone, I decided to tell somebody. I leaned over to my friend and said to her, "You know, I have visions and to prove it I am going to tell you the vision I just had." I told her and only her. …

## TWO HOURS LATER

It's the third inning and to tell you the truth, I don't even know who was up to bat. All I know is in that third inning, someone smacked the ball right out to where we were sitting in the stands. I mean right to us!!! So close I stood up and raised my hands ready to catch that ball. It was not meant to be! Literally, the gentleman behind me caught the ball. At this point, both my friend and I were freaking out. She yelled at me! "Why didn't you catch the ball? Why didn't you catch the ball?" I replied that my vision wasn't about me catching the ball, only that a ball was going to be hit up to us tonight. Our other two friends had no idea what we were so freaked out about other than the ball being hit out to us, which is exciting at any ball game! I then explained to them my vision. They were just as dumbfounded. How did you know they asked? My reply...
"I KNOW THINGS!"

---
40 ---

# THE SCARY ROCK

"AND ABOVE ALL, WATCH with glittering eyes the whole world around you because the greatest secrets are always hidden in the most unlikely places. Those who don't believe in magic will never find it"

~ ROALD DAHL

**B**EFORE I DECIDED TO GET DIVORCED, I rented a cottage in Rhode Island near the beach for the summer.

One weekend, two of my friends came with their two boys and stayed with my daughter and me. The kids spent the entire weekend body surfing. Every so often we'd make them get out of the water and take a break. They would walk to go get some ice cream at the nearby stand or they would take a walk down to the next beach that was just covered in rocks. That weekend they spent quite a bit of time down at that rock beach. My daughter is a huge rock collector like me, and she came back with a nice pile of rocks to take home. She dropped her pile next to my beach bag and off the kids went back body surfing. Inspecting all of the rocks that she brought back, I noticed one of the rocks was perfectly oval, smooth and beautiful. As I turned it over in my hand, I noticed it had a very scary face on it. I showed it to my friend and told her that rock would not be coming home with us! It was very creepy and obviously had some bad juju going on. At the end of the day as we were collecting all of our beach towels and whatnot, I gathered up the rocks except for the scary Rock. I REPEAT, NOT THE SCARY ROCK! My friend looked at me and said, "Are you sure you're not going to take that rock?" No way was I bringing that rock home. It was clearly bad juju! So I left it on the beach. I REPEAT, I LEFT IT ON THE BEACH! ...

# TWO MONTHS LATER

It was a lovely September weekend that was going to be exceptionally warm, so we decided to go camping in Rhode Island. My daughter, my husband, and I. Because the campground was close to the beaches, you could get into the beach for free when camping at the campground. On Sunday, we spent the entire day at the beach. Now, the beach that we went to was two beaches over from the beach where my daughter and I spent the whole summer. At one point during the day, I decided to take a walk down the beach, nose to the ground looking for treasures, sea glass, shells, and interesting rocks. Now this beach was very smooth and sandy. It never had rocks, shells or sea glass, ever. That never stopped me from looking. I always searched, just in case some treasure appeared. Then I spied a beautiful perfectly oval smooth rock. I immediately picked it up in my hand, and as I turned it over and looked at the other side of it, what do you think I saw? I saw a scary face! Not just any scary face, but the scary face of the rock that my daughter had found two months before, two beaches over, that we had left on the beach. I repeat , WE LEFT ON THE BEACH! It was, in fact, the very same rock! Well, I tell you I just about fell over. I looked hard at this rock, over and over and thought to myself, "How, how did this rock get to this beach, two beaches over and two months later?! How?" I asked myself. I still ask myself 20 years later… "HOW?!"

Later that day as we were in the car riding home, I pulled the rock out and showed it to my daughter. She looked surprised. I asked her, "Do you remember this rock?" She said, "Yes, I do, the scary rock!" "And I left it on the beach that day, right?" She said, "You're right, Mom, you did leave it on the beach that day!" Then she asked where I got it? I told her I found it on the beach earlier that day. She looked at me very strangely. Now mind you, she was only seven years old at the time. Did she pick up that rock a few months ago thinking that I accidentally left it behind and threw it in my bag that day? Still didn't explain how it got on that beach. Had someone actually taken the rock home with us without me knowing? Did they take it out of my bag and place it on the beach that day without me seeing? Actually, that was something my then-husband would have done. When we went sea-glassing together, he always walked behind me. When I missed a good piece, he would pick it up and throw it up ahead of me when I wasn't paying attention so I would find it and be excited about the good find. He never fessed up about the rock, which leads me to question again, "HOW!?" Whatever the reason or how it got on that beach that day is still a mystery. But, after that, the rock came home with me. It has a special guarded place in my treasure box.

I believe now, 20 years later as I write this, that all of my bad luck during that time was due to the bad juju in this scary rock. Now, I can't help but ask myself why I kept the rock the second time. The first time I knew better and left it at the beach, but the second time? I guess I felt there was a purpose, a mystery to unravel about why this rock came back to me. I've thought long and hard over this: Taking it home served as proof of the event. I really don't need the rock anymore. I have the story in this memoir, and I have the photo I took of this rock for reference... So, right after I got the perfect picture, I tossed the scary rock back into the ocean where it should've stayed in the first place. Bye-bye, bad juju! Free at last!

*Chapter* VII

# Hairtastrophy

"**HAIRGICIAN** ~ A person who can create hair magic for their clients without waving a wand."

~ *UNKNOWN*

# FACE IT... WE HAVE ALL HAD THEM!

Remember "Sun-in"? Oh yeah, that is where it all started. I have had long blonde hair pretty much my whole life. When I was 19, my friends decided to give my long blonde hair a perm. We used the wrong size rollers and it ended up being a very big afro. There was nothing anybody could do. I wore my hair in a bun for two months with lots of hair oil on it until it finally relaxed.

My best hair story happened to me when I was in my early 40s and newly divorced. I was going on a first date that night so my ex-husband was there taking care of our daughter while I went out. Thank goodness! Upstairs getting ready, I blew dry my hair, and I rolled it all onto my big fat round brush. I attached a clip to it and hit it with my blow dryer. I let it sit for about 15 minutes. It always gave my hair a nice lift and a little bend at the end. That day I had decided to go out and buy a new round brush. They didn't have one exactly like the one I had, but I bought another one thinking there was no big difference. This one had little tiny balls on the end of every bristle while the one I originally had did not. At the time, I didn't realize this could be a potential problem.

I got dressed, put on my makeup and was ready for the last and final prep, my hair. I went to unroll it and a little bit of the brush came out. Then it got stuck. I jiggled it. I rolled it back up. It got even more stuck! I worked at it and I worked at it and I worked at it, but the brush was not coming out. It was getting worse! At that point, I was severely freaking out. As a last resort I got into the shower and put a ton of conditioner on that area thinking that the hairbrush would slip out of The Rat's Nest. That did not work at all. Now, not only did I have a hairbrush stuck in my hair, I was soaking wet. Very distressed at this point, I made a 9-1-1 call to my hairdresser. Mind you, this was Friday night and the salon is slammed with customers. Panicked, I was able to reach my hairdresser and explain my dire situation.

Her response was that if I came down there right then and there she had about 15 minutes to fit me in and would see what she could do. I seriously had to drive down to the salon to get this hair brush out? She couldn't come to my house and do it? Nope, not in the cards. I had to go to the salon. ...

### FIVE MINUTES LATER

Putting on an oversized button-down shirt with hair brush sticking out of the back of my head, I drove to the salon. I got out of my car and went to go in the door. About that time, a woman was coming out of the door. I held it open for her and when she saw the hairbrush she gave me a very horrified look. I told her the next time she thought she was having a bad hair day to think about me. Only jokes were my friends at this point. I walked into the salon that was fully packed, luckily all women. Nobody looked at me, not even the hairdressers. I sat down and my hairdresser got to work.

About this time a guy friend of mine plopped down into the chair next to me. He took one look at me and trying not to laugh said, "Hey there, how are you doing? What's up?" My reply: "Oh, I'm doing just fine," because we all really know what "fine" means, right? I had hit my low point. My hairbrush was not budging. She did get some of it untangled. Enough to cut the brush out of my hair without leaving too much of a dent and not having to cut it into a pixie.

She pushed me out the door and said she would see me tomorrow at my house and give me a haircut. Lucky for me, my package store is in the same plaza as my hairdresser. I walked over to the package store and pointed to the nippers," Give me the strongest one!" I'm friends with the owner of the package store, and she looked at me very strangely and she asked me what was wrong. I turned around and showed her the back of my head. She gave me my second horrified look of the day. I looked at her and said, "Well, I guess I'm going to get those layers that my hairdresser refused to cut into my hair." And that's the truth of it, cuz I did want layers in my hair for a very long time. She wouldn't do it. Now she was forced to.

Side note: If you can't get your hairdresser to cut layers into your hair, get a hairbrush stuck in it. Make her cut it out and give you layers. I got the best haircut of my life after getting that hairbrush stuck in my hair. Sure, I had a little bit of a dent in the back for about a month, but she did such a good job covering it up… with the layers! Nobody ever noticed, and in fact, I got a lot of compliments.

As far as my date? I did have to cancel. That's okay, he was a dud, anyway!

🦎

*Chapter* VIII

# April Fools

"IT'S IN THEIR EYES that their magic resides."

~ *ARTHUR SYMONS*

*A*T ONE TIME IN MY LIFE, I was known as the crazy divorced cat lady. It all started out innocently and quickly escalated out of control. It happened so fast!

I am a fierce animal lover, and I detest when people dump animals or leave them behind. I live in a condo complex and this happens quite often. This is how I adopted one of my cats. It's so heartbreaking.

This happened to a family that lived two doors down from me. It started off innocently. They had two female cats that they just decided to let outside and roam freely and not be fixed. This is where the madness started. They got pregnant, not once, not twice, but quite a few times. It was a vicious circle. But somehow most of the kittens got adopted until the last four. The family moved and left four kittens. They were about 6 months old. Most of them found their own homes and were adopted by people in the complex, thank goodness. I adopted the cute little Calico girl cat. Little did I know at the time she was pregnant. She had three kittens. I gave away one and kept two. And here's where things started to go very wrong. This little sassy girl loved to be outside and she loved to go hunting. I could not keep her inside. Before I could get her fixed, she escaped and I couldn't get her back in. When she did come back in, I learned she'd gotten herself knocked up! ...

Sitting down to have a fresh cup of coffee one morning, after dropping my daughter off at school, this sassy little calico girl got in my face. She meowed at me very loudly and was very anxious. I took one look at her and realized she must have had her kittens and something was wrong. I told her to show me where her kittens were, and off she ran to show me. To my surprise, she revealed one little kitten who did not look well at all. I called the vet immediately and explained what was going on, and they told me to get Mom and her kitten in as fast as I could. When I arrived at the vet, they took the crate right from me and told me to sit in the waiting room. I sat and waited for the verdict. As I sat there waiting and praying, I realized it was none other than April Fool's Day! Of course this crazy stuff is happening to me on April Fool's Day! This is my life! A friend of mine once told me that my life was like a country music song, and it totally is.

The veterinarian came out to speak with me and told me that they hydrated the little kitten and it seemed to be doing better. But there was another kitten stuck inside the mama. She would have to have a cesarean to get the kitten out. A cesarean? Really? I have never heard of that before, so obviously I thought it was an April Fool's joke. I looked at the veterinarian and said, "April fools, right?" At this point he gave me a very stern look and said "No, this is not an April Fool's joke! This is really what's happening. And if she doesn't have a cesarean, you will lose her and the kitten inside her!" Shocked over all of this news, I, of course said, "Yes, perform this cesarean and while you're in there, can you fix her too?" A few hours later I had two kittens and a mama that was fixed, and we went home. Unfortunately, the first little kitten passed away, but this little ball of fat chubby fur of the other kitten was alive and well. My daughter and I named him Chubby, and we decided to keep him. I seriously don't know what I was thinking. I already had five cats! This cat ended up being my best friend, my constant companion, the biggest bully in the house, and I loved the crap out of him.

Out of crazy madness came a ball of fur that was my heart. I say "was" because he tragically passed two days before I moved to Tennessee. I have, to this day, never gotten over it. One by one, all my cats went over the rainbow bridge. When my last one went, I was relieved on many levels; the vet bills, flying cat fur, and gifted dead animals. You get it, pet ownership, but I was very lonely. One month later, a cute little kitten became available. A male the same sex and color as Chubby except for the white stripe down his nose. I decided to throw caution to the wind and adopt him. Ironically, he has Chubby's personality and likes. Chubby was obsessed with straws, loved maple syrup, and got crazy wild jumping under the covers when I made the bed. So does Blaze. He is my constant companion since day one, and I swear he is Chubby reincarnated! When it was his time to cross the rainbow bridge, I told Chubby that he had to come back to me. Four years after his death, to the week, Blaze came into the world and into my world on Friday the 13th, my lucky number. So… hmmm… is he really Chubby? I think he is, and I'm going to tell you why: Chubby was the last one born of all my cats, and he had to share me with them, and he hated that. That's why he bullied all the other cats in the house. He waited for the last one to die when he knew darn well coming back he'd be my one and only fur love. And he totally is.

❧

*Chapter* IX

## ROSES FOR MRS. CLAUS

"CHILDREN SEE MAGIC

because they look for it."

~ CHRISTOPHER MOORE

*I* HAVE WORKED SEVERAL RETAIL JOBS over the years. At one point, I worked at a flower and gift shop. The owner, my boss, hired me to manage the shop while she took a job out of town during the week. Working with me was our part-time florist who came in and did the major floral design work, and I pinch-hit when I could with small arrangements. On this particularly hot summer day in July, she was there with her eight-year-old daughter. At the time, we were candidly complaining about a situation at work when a customer dropped in. ...

## A SPLIT SECOND LATER

When what to our wondering eyes did appear? ... A little old man so lively and quick. He was jolly and round with a long white beard, a red t-shirt, suspenders, and jeans. We thought to ourselves instantly it must be Saint Nick! At that moment, the florist's daughter's eyes got big and round and under her breath she said, "It's Santa!" She said exactly what we were thinking.

The man came to the counter and asked if we had any red roses. Of course, we assumed they were for Mrs. Claus. As the florist was wrapping up his roses and I was cashing him out, he saw our lineup of penny candy in front of the register. For some reason, we still had candy canes out in the middle of July. This delighted the gentleman aka Santa Claus. He was very excited that we still had the candy canes out and remarked that they were his favorite brand. All the while my eight-year-old friend was just in awe! As he gathered his flowers and was about to leave, he turned to my eight-year-old friend and with a twinkle in his eye asked her, "Have you been a good little girl so far this year?" Her reply further melted us on that hot summer day. "Why yes, Santa! I have. Thank you for asking." And with that, laying a finger aside his nose, a sparkle in his eye, a twist of his head and giving us a nod, out the door he sprang.

What in the world just happened?! Did Santa just come and visit us in July? WE MET SANTA! We were left speechless! We felt so special!

We imagined that Santa was vacationing at one of our local camp-grounds because you know, Santa works hard and he needs a vacation too! Instead of a sleigh and eight tiny reindeer, he would be driving a 700-horsepower bright red Chevy pickup truck towing an Airstream.

*Chapter* x

# CHRISTMAS EVE MIRACLE

"**MAGIC CAN BE FOUND** in stolen moments."

*~ FRANCESCA LIA BLOCK*

*I* WAS ASKED BY A FRIEND OF MINE to attend the Christmas Eve candlelight service at her church with her daughter. Now mind you, I am NOT a church goer at all. But this church is a very old historic church down by the Connecticut River, and I thought to myself, how wonderful to spend Christmas Eve at such a beautiful place. So I said yes, knowing full-well the sinner that I am.

On Christmas Eve morning, I always run to the grocery store to pick up Italian bread for my Italian strata that I make the day ahead for Christmas morning. It requires fresh Italian bread. It is always such a delight to run into the grocery store on Christmas Eve. Everyone is usually Merry and bright. Not this Christmas Eve. Everybody was grumpy, in a big hurry and inpatient. Very Scrooge-like! I noticed this while standing in line and waiting to be cashed out, and it made me kind of sad. Just then a gentleman behind me leaned over and said, "They just don't get it." Did this man just read my mind? I exclaimed, "Seriously, it's Christmas Eve! Everyone should be joyful!" We then ended up having a very nice conversation while waiting in line. When I was done, I turned, said my goodbyes and bid, "Happy Holidays!"

When my daughter arrived home from college that day, she asked what we were doing that night. I told her we had been invited to go to church with our friends. Her eyes got big and her mouth fell open. "Those are words I thought would never come out of your mouth, Mom!" Unlike myself, my daughter is a church-goer who had attended church many times with her grandmother. I laughed and said, "Listen, as soon as my feet hit the steps of that church, lightning is going to strike me!" ...

## THREE HOURS LATER

Our friends picked us up and off we went to church. In the car, I warned them all about the fact that I'm a sinner and told them to not stand too close to me when we entered the church because lightning was going to strike me. Everyone thought it was so funny, but I was kinda serious. As we got out of the car, I warned them again to go ahead of me just in case of the lightning. When I got to the steps of the church, a person was handing out programs and greeting everyone as they entered. As I reached that spot and looked up to take the program from this person's hand, I realized at that moment it was none other than the gentleman that I was in line with at the grocery store. We looked at each other with surprise and delight. I exclaimed, "Nice to see you again!"

### *Lighting Strike Number One:*

As it turned out, he was the Reverend of the church. I entered the church, all candlelit and Christmassy, feeling so blessed and loved by God at that moment. Like He was trying to tell me something. I sat down and said nothing to the rest of our party about what just happened.

*Lighting Strike Number Two:*

To my surprise the sermon started out by the Reverend saying to the congregation, "They just don't get it! I sat through the rest of that service so dumbfounded. It was the most wonderful Christmas Eve ever! There was even snow on the ground!

Still in awe on the ride home, I said nothing to anyone until I arrived home with my daughter. After we settled down to a plate of Christmas cookies, I said "I have a magical Christmas Eve story for you." I told her about my day and pointed out how it connected with what happened that evening. At the end of my story, I stopped and reminded her of how tonight's sermon started with "THEY JUST DON'T GET IT!" She looked at me and exclaimed, "WOW! Lightning did strike! Twiced! Lighting struck twiced! It was our little funny southern word we liked to use every chance we got. Boy, did it fit in in that moment. You'd be surprised how many times "twice" comes up in daily conversation!

Never underestimate the power of God. He works in mysterious ways.

# Chapter XI

## Lady In The Blue Dress

"IT'S ALL A MATTER OF PAYING ATTENTION, being awake in the present moment, and not expecting a huge payoff. The magic in this world seems to work in whispers and small kindnesses.

~ CHARLES DE LINT

*I*N LIFE, YOU SOMETIMES DON'T LEARN your lesson the first time!

At the age of 56, I sold everything and moved to Tennessee where I lived for just over a year. I was going to start a flower and herb farm on my grandparents' property and build a tree house on a portion of the land I inherited. During that year, everything that could go wrong certainly did. It was a lonely year. Full of disappointment. And my flower and herb farm idea went out the door. I originally was going to live in my grandparents' house, that my brother now owned, while I set up shop and built on my property. That did not work out, so I moved down the mountain to a cottage on Lake Chickamauga and got myself a therapist. I kept myself sane by gardening at my new little place while I figured out what I was going to do next. I was so lost in a place where I only knew two people.

On a particularly hot day, I drove over to Lowe's to scope out all the annuals on sale. Of course, I did not leave empty handed! While in line to cash out, (what is it with me and people standing in line?!) I noticed the woman in front of me wearing a very pretty sundress. Turquoise eyelet with a green underskirt. She looked so cute in it! After cashing out, but before she left, I spoke up and complimented her on her dress and told her she looked pretty in it. She turned to me and gave me a weird look and thanked me. Hmmm that was weird. No smile, no nothing. Just a weird look and barely a thank you. Was it my Northern accent? Did she think I was hitting on me? I really could not figure out her reaction. I shook it off and went about my day. ...

## ONE MONTH LATER

Thrifting was another way I kept sane while in Tennessee. Oh, the treasures I found! We had a wonderful thrift store in the same plaza as my grocery store. I was in there at least three days a week looking for gold. I really never looked at the clothing section. I was there for the vintage stuff! But on this particular day, a sign caught my eye. Sundresses $5.00. Who could pass that up? I went over and started flipping through the rack when my eyes caught a glimpse of a turquoise eyelet dress with a green underskirt! The very dress the woman at Lowe's was wearing. I could not believe it! Man, she must have been so creeped out by my compliment that she gave the dress away. It made me a bit sad, but also happy! I really did like that dress. It was my size and an Anne Taylor to boot! You know what? I bought it! I could not pass up that deal. But this is not the end of the story with this dress. ...

## ANOTHER MONTH LATER

I realized, like my Mom, it was time for this New England Yankee to move back home to Connecticut. What I went to Tennessee to accomplish was never going to happen. Defeated, I made my plan to get the heck outta there!

Several days before moving, I went down to our electric utility company to pay my final bill and have my electricity turned off. I was called into the office. Sitting behind the desk was none other than the lady from Lowe's, and she was wearing the turquoise dress! I had to take a few minutes to shake my head and look again to make sure I wasn't seeing things. But sure enough it was her! She asked what she could help me with. I said, "First off, let's talk about your dress! Do you remember being complimented on that dress one day when you were in Lowe's? That was me!" She smiled and did remember. I told her I thought she was creeped out about my compliment and that she must have given the dress away, and how I bought it. She explained that she rarely ever gets compliments and it just kinda threw her off that day. She said, "Do you know that is an Anne Taylor? I paid full price for it. How much did you pay?" I hated to tell her it was only five dollars. She also informed me that they had a pink one with an orange underskirt! I have been on the hunt for that one ever since. The funny part of this was, I was going to wear that dress that day! Now, wouldn't that have been cool and maybe a little creepy?!

As I prepared to drive back to Connecticut by myself, my two cats, and all my plants, I was glad to end my time in Tennessee on a good note. My mom said to me over the phone that I needed to find myself a Hardee's, go inside, get dinner and sit down on the sunny side of the restaurant. Maybe a motorcycle man would be there waiting for me.

# AFTERWARD

_Chapter_ XII

# Magic Creates Magic

# "MAGIC HAPPENS!

It always shows up when you need it the most"

~ *MINDY MILLS MAYNARD*

*A*FTER WRITING THIS BOOK and in the process of publishing it, magic started happening. So I knew I was on the right track.

One day on our Town Facebook page someone asked, "who is that gentleman that dresses up as Santa Claus and drives around in the bright red antique car?" A woman answered the post and said it was her father. I immediately knew it was the gentleman that had come in to buy the roses the day I was working at the store. I quickly contacted her and told her about this book and about the story written about her father. I told her I wanted to meet him and share my story. Sifting through much confusion, we were finally able to connect and we met at a local McDonald's of all places! This gentleman told me all about his story of being Santa Claus. As it turns out, he is the brother of one of the owners of the garden center that hands out my business cards for my gardening business. Coincidence? I think not! ...

## SEVERAL WEEKS LATER

I decided that I wanted to be photographed wearing the dress that my grandmother danced with General Patton in. And I thought about having it altered because it was way too big on me now as I am 20 pounds lighter than I was when I first tried it on over 20 years ago. Simultaneously, I had an alternate plan in mind and contacted the World War II museum in New Orleans to donate the dress. I met with a seamstress, who happened to be the daughter of an artist friend of mine. Her specialty is vintage clothing. When I went to her house to bring her the dress, I sat in her living room and talked with her for three hours. When I got back into my car I couldn't believe three hours had gone by. It was like meeting an old friend and I had never met this woman before in my life. We had an instant connection.

As it turns out, I decided not to have the dress altered in any way and not to be photographed in it. When I went to retrieve the dress and stepping over to my car to open my car door, there was a penny heads up. It was not there when I got out of my car. But it was there waiting for me when I got back to my car. Coincidence? I think not. ...

## SEVERAL MORE WEEKS LATER

While gathering my artwork for this book, I came across a painting that I did when I was 13. A watercolor of a tree. I threw it into the mix. I met with my graphic designer the next day showing her the potential art that would be going into the book when she spotted the painting of the tree. She then asked, "Did you do this painting after you moved here when you were 23?" I looked at her very strangely and said no I did this when I was 13. She looked at me very astonished and exclaimed, "Mindy, this is the tree that is down at your beach and the cover of your book… right down to the spot where hurricane Gloria broke off that branch. I looked at her hard and then I looked at the painting. I could not believe my eyes. It was almost the exact same tree. That shook me up pretty hard. Just so I didn't think that both of us were crazy, I sent a photo of the painting to my daughter and to a good friend of mine and ask them this, "where have you seen this tree before?" Without hesitation they both said, "That's the tree from the beach."

So at age 13 in the back of my mind or my subconscious knew this tree was going to play a major part in my life… 10 solid years before I ever saw it? Coincidence? I think not!

Which leads me to believe there's a higher being. And my faith in the higher being is stronger than ever. Never stop believing in magic. Magic happens when the chips are down, the stakes are high and you're down to your last dime… magic steps in. Every story in this book happened to me when I was struggling with something in my life. But these magical things happened amidst chaos, making them even more special. They brought me out of deep places and helped me to realize there's more to this life and I need to keep living it and keep moving forward. So if I leave you with nothing else, know that magic exist and is all around us all the time shining like glitter. It's there for the taking, so open up your eyes, your heart and your arms…. REACH OUT AND GRAB IT!

## ABOUT THE ARTWORK

THE ARTWORK CHOSEN FOR THIS BOOK is from my fifty plus years of creating art. I'm a multimedia artist with works in watercolors, fine pencil and colored pencil, sea glass mosaics and driftwood creations.

I chose to keep a theme throughout the book so I chose only paintings that I did of flowers. Except for the tree painting. Since flowers have always been a theme in my life, that was the theme I chose for this book. I didn't just want to tell my stories. I wanted to also show you another piece of my story through my artwork. Special thanks to R.J. Phil for beautifully photographing my illustrations and Cheryl Gioielli for bringing my vision to life.

## A *special message* FROM MINDY

A secret message is concealed inside this book. You may have noticed twelve colorful words scattered throughout the text. They are not typos. Beginning with chapter one, arrange the colorful words in order to reveal a magical message from me.

# ABOUT THE AUTHOR

**M**INDY MILLS MAYNARD is a mother, multimedia nature artist and professional gardener living in the magical small town of East Hampton, Connecticut just steps from Lake Pocotopaug with her sweet rescue cat Blaze.

My book is dedicated to helping animal rescue groups that are near and dear to my heart all over our country. Please consider donating to one of these groups or one in your area. I will be donating a small portion of the proceeds from the sales of this book.

**PASSION 4 PAWS:**
Dayville, CT
Passion4Paws.org

**PURPLE ARK PACK:**
East Hampton, CT
PurpleArkRescue@gmail.com

**PROTECTORS OF ANIMALS:**
144 Main Street
East Hartford ,CT
poainc.org

**A PLACE CALLED HOPE:**
154 Pond Meadow Road
Killingworth, CT
aplacecalledhoperaptors.com

**THE GENTLE BARN:**
gentlebarn.org

**THE ASHER HOUSE:**
TheAsherHouse.com

**CATS OF SAN BERNARDINO:**
catsofsanbernardino.org

## YOU CAN MAGICALLY FIND ME ON:

**INSTAGRAM:**
@3Martandgardenworks
@WhenMagicHappens_TheBook

**EMAIL:** mindymills@gmail.com

## SPECIAL THANKS TO —

Donna Koropatkin

Jack Matthews

Cheryl Gioielli

Ralph (R.J.) Phil

Without all of you, I could not have
accomplished this work of art.

www.ingramcontent.com/pod-product-compliance
Lightning Source LLC
Chambersburg PA
CBRC090837120626
46551CB00007B/688